EDGE
BOOKS

SCARY STORIES

SCARY
FOLKTALES

BY MEGAN KOPP

Consultant:
Simon J. Bronner, PhD
Distinguished Professor of American Studies and Folklore
Fellow, American Folklore Society
The Pennsylvania State University, Harrisburg

CAPSTONE PRESS
a capstone imprint

Edge Books are published by Capstone Press,
151 Good Counsel Drive, P.O. Box 669, Mankato, Minnesota 56002.
www.capstonepub.com

Library of Congress Cataloging-in-Publication Data
Kopp, Megan.
 Scary folktales / by Megan Kopp.
  p. cm.—(Edge books. Scary stories)
 Summary: In this collection of spine-tingling tales, a woman encounters a deadly box
full of eyeballs and a boy watches as a princess takes off her head.
 Includes bibliographical references and index.
 ISBN 978-1-4296-4571-3 (library binding)
 1. Tales. 2. Horror tales. [1. Folklore. 2. Horror stories.] I. Title.
PZ8.1.K755Sc 2011
398.2—dc22   2010001683

Editorial Credits
Megan Peterson, editor; Ted Williams, designer; Kelly Garvin, media researcher;
    Laura Manthe, production specialist

Photo Credits
Capstone Studio/Karon Dubke, scaremeter, 13, 28
Dreamstime/Alen Dobric, 23; Boumenjapet, 24; Elena Ray, 4; Vgrzinic, 10; Yuriy
    Mazur, 15
Fotolia/Vedmochka, 8
iStockphoto/Andrew Johnson, 21; Dmitry Mordolff, 26; SigridJnsson, cover;
Shutterstock/Andrei Merkulov, 7; Eric Isselee, 17; Laurin Rinder, 18; Losevsky
    Pavel, 16

Design Elements
Shutterstock/averole (hand prints), Charles Taylor (rusty background), David M.
    Schrader (paper w/tape), DCD (dribbles), Eugene Ivanov (border), George Nazmi
    Bebawi (fly), Gordan (borders), Hal_P (fingerprints), hfng (word bubble), Ian
    O'Ha (spider web), Kirsty Pargeter (brush strokes border), oxygen64 (frames),
    Ralf Juergen Kraft (computer bug), silver-john (paper), Subbotina Anna (fly),
    Thomas Bethge (tapes), xjbxjhxm123 (button)

TABLE OF CONTENTS

TELLING TALES

L ight from a fire flickers across a cave, and shadows dance wildly against the stone. A man walks slowly around the circle of young and old gathered near the fire. He has a story to share. As he speaks, his words echo in the dark chamber. No one dares to breathe. By the time he's done telling his scary tale, no one will want to head outside alone.

Storytelling has been around for thousands of years. Folktales are made-up stories about people or animals. They are passed on by word of mouth from one **generation** to the next.

Because folktales are **oral** stories, it is almost impossible to know how old they are. But many folktales were eventually written down in books. *Grimm's Fairy Tales*, first published in 1812, is a famous collection of German folktales.

Folktales can be funny, sad, or scary. And they don't always have happy endings. The folktales in this book are creepy enough to send chills running down your spine. Are you brave enough to read on?

generation—all members of a group of people born around the same time
oral—spoken

Fear Fact

A fairy tale is a type of folktale. But fairy tales don't always include fairies. Scholars prefer to label these stories as wonder or marvel tales.

AN ICY END
A RUSSIAN FOLKTALE

SCARY

Mary worked from dawn to dusk washing floors, making beds, and cooking meals. But no matter how hard Mary worked, she couldn't please her stepmother. One day, Mary's stepmother sent her out alone to a distant, snow-covered field to gather wood. She didn't even give Mary a cloak for warmth.

The bitter cold soon made Mary weak, and she huddled beneath a fir tree. Suddenly ice sprayed from the sky like broken glass. King Frost appeared on his sleigh. "Are you cold, maiden?" King Frost bellowed.

"I'm quite warm, your highness," Mary answered through blue lips. The cold wind felt like a thousand tiny needles stabbing her skin.

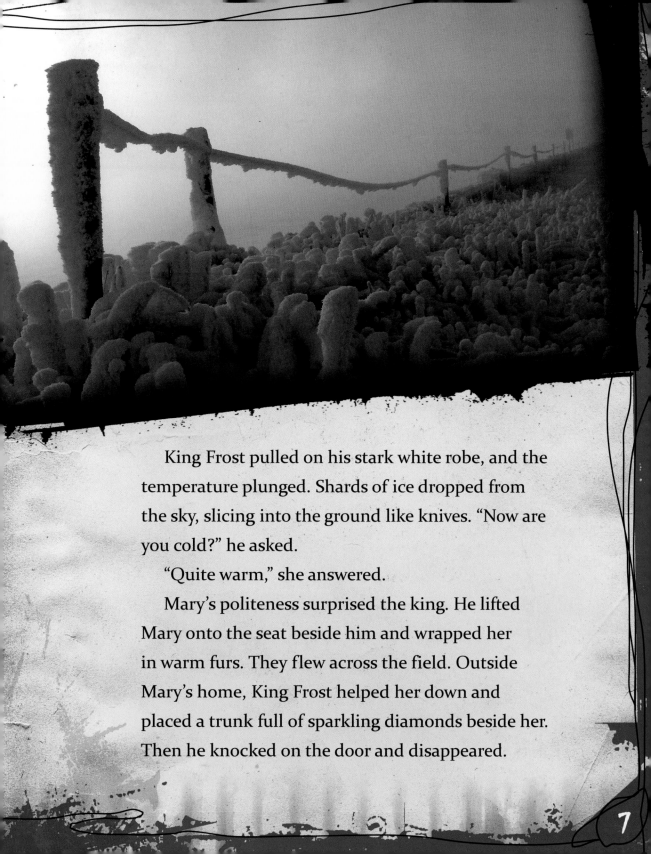

King Frost pulled on his stark white robe, and the temperature plunged. Shards of ice dropped from the sky, slicing into the ground like knives. "Now are you cold?" he asked.

"Quite warm," she answered.

Mary's politeness surprised the king. He lifted Mary onto the seat beside him and wrapped her in warm furs. They flew across the field. Outside Mary's home, King Frost helped her down and placed a trunk full of sparkling diamonds beside her. Then he knocked on the door and disappeared.

Fear Fact

Cryophobia is the fear of cold and ice. People with cryophobia often dress in heavy clothing, live in hot climates, and avoid eating cold foods.

The stepmother opened the door. She was shocked to find Mary covered in thick furs and carrying a chest full of diamonds. The stepmother quickly wrapped her own daughter in a thick cloak and sent her to the same field.

As the daughter waited in the ice-cold snow, King Frost appeared in a flurry of pelting hail. "Give me diamonds and furs and take me home," the girl demanded. "And make it quick. I'm freezing."

"Freezing, are you?" shouted the king. Icy mountains rose out of the field like swords. A bitterly cold wind rattled the trees.

"Stop that right now," the girl roared back. "I want my reward!"

That was when King Frost snapped his fingers, and the girl instantly froze to death. When the stepmother found her daughter in the field, a deadly chill also passed through her body. Since then, the field turns red just before the snow falls.

BAD VIBES
A BRITISH FOLKTALE

SCARY

The market was crowded and noisy. Caged birds squawked, and mice scurried under the stalls. A mother told her two daughters to pick up a loaf of bread and come straight home. But the sisters couldn't resist a young girl wrapped in a cloak. A wooden dragon with glass eyes hung from the chain wrapped around her neck. But it was the music box the girl held that really drew the sisters in. Wooden figures of a boy and girl whirled around and around as the music played. The sisters begged the girl to give them the music box.

"You can have it," the girl said. "But only if you are bad for one day."

That night the sisters complained about their dinner. They argued about bedtime and refused to kiss their mother good night.

"You have not been bad enough," the girl told the sisters the next day. "Try again."

This time the sisters threw food at each other across the table. They stepped on the dog's tail and pinched their mother's arm.

"If you continue to behave badly," their mother warned, "I may have to go away. And you will be stuck with another mother. She might have a wooden tail and glass eyes that can't see how good you can be."

When the sisters met the girl again, they were sure they had earned the music box. But the girl was not impressed. She explained that the music box was magical. They must be very bad to deserve it.

The sisters ran home and hid in the barn. They didn't answer when their mother called their names. When she left to find them, the sisters emptied a sack of flour all over the kitchen. They danced with glee, certain they had been bad enough to earn the magical music box.

A sharp knock on the door snapped them to attention. "Who's there?" the sisters asked.

"Your new mother!" a voice croaked.

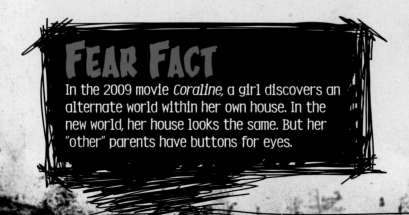

FEAR FACT

In the 2009 movie *Coraline*, a girl discovers an alternate world within her own house. In the new world, her house looks the same. But her "other" parents have buttons for eyes.

The door burst open and fell from its hinges. The girl from the market dropped her cloak, and her wooden tail fell to the ground with a thud. As she stepped inside, her glass eyes glowed.

The sisters were never seen or heard from again. But their new mother's glass eyes can still be seen glowing through the windows of the house.

Headed for Trouble
A Russian Folktale

Very Scary

Walking home from school one afternoon, a young boy passed by a large castle. He looked up at one of the castle windows and was horrified by what he saw. The princess sat down at her dressing table and took off her head. She washed the long black hair, rinsed it, and pulled it into a braid. Then the princess put her head back on her neck and slowly turned her head. She stared out the window directly at the boy.

"A witch!" the boy thought as he stumbled on a loose stone. He couldn't wait to tell everyone what he had seen.

The next day, thick gray clouds swirled around the towering castle. The princess was dying. She made the king promise that he would find the boy. She wanted the boy to read a prayer over her body the night before she was buried.

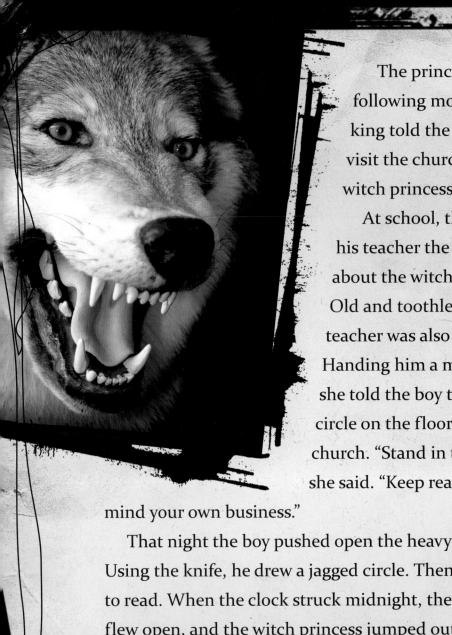

The princess died the following morning. The king told the boy he must visit the church where the witch princess lay dead.

At school, the boy told his teacher the twisted tale about the witch princess. Old and toothless, the teacher was also a witch. Handing him a magic knife, she told the boy to carve a circle on the floor inside the church. "Stand in the circle," she said. "Keep reading and mind your own business."

That night the boy pushed open the heavy church door. Using the knife, he drew a jagged circle. Then he started to read. When the clock struck midnight, the coffin lid flew open, and the witch princess jumped out.

Fear Fact

The practice of drawing magical circles has been around for centuries. Some people believe the circle has the power to keep away bad spirits.

"I'll teach you to talk about me!" she hissed. Bolts of lightning flew from her fingertips. The boy kept his eyes down and whispered the words from the book. The magical circle held. The princess became a spitting cobra that went round and round the circle. But she could not reach the boy. She turned into a wolf and howled in madness. Still, the circle held.

As the sun rose, a ray of light touched the blood-red glass on one of the church windows. The light struck the princess, and she dropped to the floor. Just as the king entered the church, her head rolled off to one side. His eyes darted from the open coffin to the headless body of the princess.

"If you never talk of what happened here, I will reward you with great riches," the king told the boy. The king thrust a wooden stake deep into the heart of the headless body. Then he placed the head and body inside the coffin and nailed the lid shut. The witch princess was gone for good. Or was she?

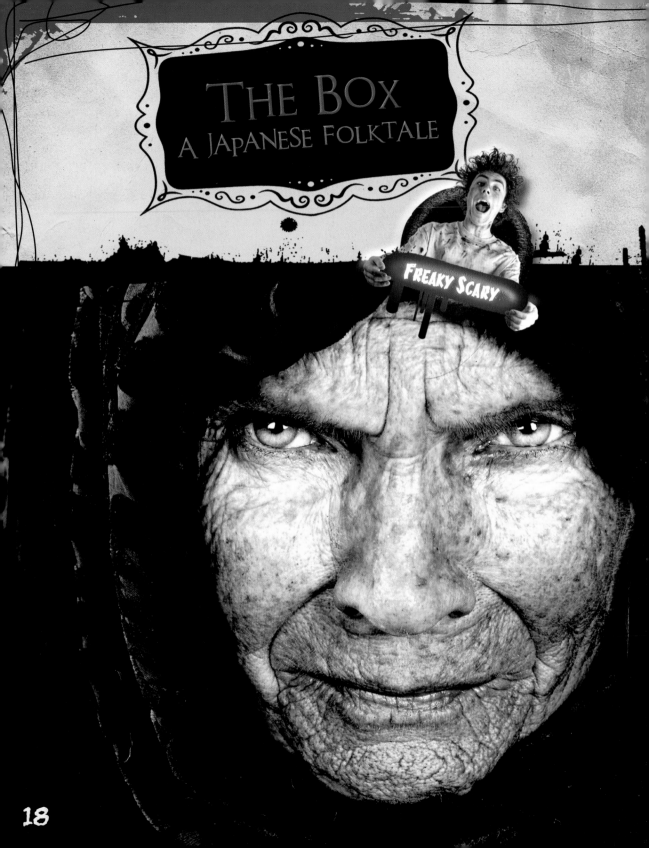

THE BOX
A JAPANESE FOLKTALE

Freaky Scary

Moonlight turned the leafless trees into ghostly figures as a man raced his horse down a path. The horse lunged forward, frothing at the mouth. The man spurred the animal on harder. He had spent months building a new temple for the emperor, and he was finally going home.

Through an opening in the trees, the man saw an arching stone bridge. He darted onto the bridge. Suddenly an old woman dressed in black appeared in his path. He jerked the horse to a stop and climbed down.

"Where are you headed?" the woman asked. The hood of her black cloak clung to her withered face.

"Home," the man replied. He tried to move around the woman, but she blocked his path.

"Would you help me?" she asked. "I need someone to take this box and leave it at the next bridge." The woman thrust a roughly carved wooden chest into the man's hands. "Whatever you do, don't open this box," she warned. "It's a matter of life and death."

The man stared for a moment at the simple dark wood and hammered metal hinges of the box. When he looked up again, the woman was gone. Shrugging, the man mounted his horse and raced home. He forgot to drop off the box.

The man's wife was waiting for his arrival. She watched him place a strange box under the bush outside their front door. Could it be a gift? When the man fell asleep, his wife crept out into the blackness. She slowly opened the lid of the box and screamed. Decaying eyeballs stared up at her.

The bloodcurdling scream woke up the man. He rushed outside, scooped up the box, and saddled his horse. Fog blanketed the path as he raced toward the bridge. Tree branches clawed at him. Out of the mist, the same old woman appeared on the bridge. The man gave her the box.

FEAR FACT

In the French folktale "Bluebeard," a man tells his new wife not to enter one room of the house. When she goes into the forbidden room, she discovers the dead bodies of her husband's previous wives.

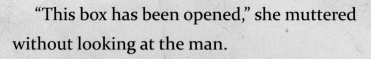

"This box has been opened," she muttered without looking at the man.

"But I never opened the box!" the man told her. The old woman didn't answer. Instead she turned, took a step, and vanished. The man stood on the bridge, shaking.

The next morning, his wife woke up to a cold companion. The man was dead. The box had claimed another victim.

GIVE IT BACK
A GERMAN FOLKTALE

FREAKY SCARY

A bone-chilling wind whipped around a run-down home. Shutters banged and walls creaked. An old woman lifted a cast-iron pot from the stove. A drop of boiling water slopped over the side of the pot and onto her bare toes. Wincing, she dumped the water into the sink.

Dinner was over, and the woman grabbed the empty plates from the table. They never needed scraping. Food was scarce, and sometimes the old woman couldn't afford to buy meat.

23

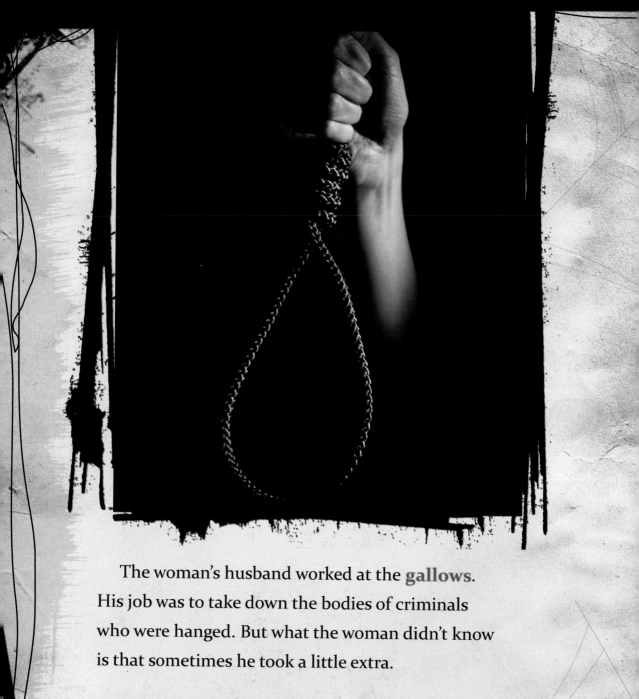

The woman's husband worked at the **gallows**.
His job was to take down the bodies of criminals
who were hanged. But what the woman didn't know
is that sometimes he took a little extra.

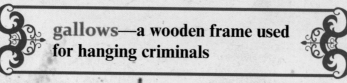

gallows—a wooden frame used
for hanging criminals

Suddenly a knock came at the door. There stood a tall, pale stranger. The man had a gash in his side where his liver had been. The old woman felt the hairs rise on the back of her neck.

"Give it back," the man croaked.

"Pardon me?"

"Give it back," he repeated.

"What do you want back?" the old woman asked. She slowly backed away from the man.

"My liver," the man said. "You ate it!"

Blood drained from the woman's face. She slammed the door shut and hobbled up the rickety stairs, calling her husband's name. Silence. She rushed into the bedroom, and there he lay with a hole where his liver should be. Gagging, she left the room.

From the top of the stairs, she heard another knock on the door.

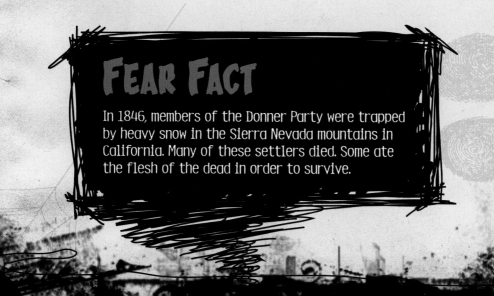

FEAR FACT

In 1846, members of the Donner Party were trapped by heavy snow in the Sierra Nevada mountains in California. Many of these settlers died. Some ate the flesh of the dead in order to survive.

FOLKTALE
TRUTHS

Different versions of the same folktales are often told in many **cultures**. Historians have found hundreds of versions of the Cinderella story in countries such as China, France, and Germany. The British folktale "The Golden Arm" is similar to the German folktale "Give It Back." In the British version, a man steals his dead wife's golden arm. The wife returns from the dead to claim the missing arm. Historians believe these stories may have spread when people traveled. It's also possible different cultures simply created the same types of stories. But it's almost impossible to know exactly when or where many folktales began.

 culture—**a people's way of life, ideas, customs, and traditions**

PERFECT YOUR SCARY STORYTELLING

Even though we know folktales are make-believe, does that make them any less creepy? Try telling one of these folktales to your friends late at night while tucked under a blanket fort. Hold a flashlight under your chin to put eerie shadows on your face. Talk slowly and softly. Pick up the pace toward the end of the tale.

Are certain words scarier than others? If you tried to describe one of these stories to someone else in 25 words or less, would it be as scary?

Here's another hint—scary stories shouldn't give it all away. Why did the box full of eyeballs kill the man? We don't need to know. Our imaginations will fill in the blanks!

GLOSSARY

culture (KUHL-chuhr)—a people's way of life, ideas, customs, and traditions

emperor (EM-puhr-uhr)—a male ruler of a country or group of countries

gallows (GAL-ohz)—a wooden frame used for hanging criminals

generation (jen-uh-RAY-shuhn)—all members of a group of people born around the same time

oral (OR-uhl)—spoken, not written

shard (SHARD)—a piece or fragment of a breakable substance such as glass or ice

spirit (SPIHR-it)—the invisible part of a person that contains thoughts and feelings; some people believe the spirit leaves the body after death

READ MORE

Olson, Arielle North, and Howard Schwartz.
More Bones: Scary Stories from around the World.
New York: Viking, 2008.

O'Shei, Tim. *Creepy Urban Legends.* Scary Stories.
Mankato, Minn.: Capstone Press, 2011.

Parkhurst, Liz, ed. *The August House Book of Scary Stories: Spooky Tales for Telling Out Loud.*
Atlanta: August House, 2009.

Teitelbaum, Michael. *The Scary States of America.*
New York: Delacorte Press, 2007.

INTERNET SITES

FactHound offers a safe, fun way to find Internet sites related to this book. All of the sites on FactHound have been researched by our staff.

Here's all you do:

Visit *www.facthound.com*

Type in this code: 9781429645713

INDEX